INSPIRING BASEBALL STORIES FOR KIDS

Fun, Inspirational Facts & Stories For Young Readers

FALCON FOCUS

Copyright © 2023 Falcon Focus

All rights reserved. No part of this publication may be reproduced, distributed or transmitted in any form or by any means, including photocopying, recording, or other electronic or mechanical methods, without the prior written permission of the publisher, except in the case of brief quotations embodied in critical reviews and certain other non-commercial uses permitted by copyright law.

Trademarked names appear throughout this book. Rather than use a trademark symbol with every occurrence of a trademarked name, names are used in an editorial fashion, with no intention of infringement of the respective owner's trademark. The information in this book is distributed on an "as is" basis, without warranty. Although every precaution has been taken in the preparation of this work, neither the author nor the publisher shall have any liability to any person or entity with respect to any loss or damage caused or alleged to be caused directly or indirectly by the information contained in this book.

Baseball is more than a sport; it's a poetic dance played out on the diamond. Each pitch is a stanza, every home run a grand finale, and every catch a delicate ballet beneath the open sky. On this field, every double play is a narrative of teamwork, every stolen base a display of speed, and every well-executed strategy a symphony of athleticism and precision. In this arena, legends emerge, perseverance is spotlighted, and every run scored is a stride toward victory etched in the fervor of both players and fans.

Contents

Introduction	v
1. Breaking Barriers: Jackie Robinson	1
2. The Miracle on Grass: 1980 US Olympic Baseball Team	8
3. The First Woman in Baseball: Jackie Mitchell	14
4. Youngest Major Leaguer: Joe Nuxhall	20
5. The Home Run Hero: Hank Aaron	26
6. The Perfect Game: Don Larsen	32
7. The Little League Phenomenon: Mo'ne Davis	38
8. The Iron Man: Cal Ripken Jr.	44
9. Baseball and Civil Rights: Roberto Clemente	50
10. Babe Ruth's Inspiring Journey	56
References	63
Bonus: Free Book!	65

Introduction

Welcome to *Inspiring Baseball Stories For Kids*, a collection that will take you on a captivating journey through the rich history of baseball. Within these pages, you'll discover the remarkable stories of individuals whose dedication, resilience, and passion for the game have left an indelible mark on the world of sports.

From breaking barriers to achieving the extraordinary, each narrative unfolds like an exciting play-by-play, offering insights into the lives of baseball legends who became symbols of inspiration and determination. These stories not only chronicle the triumphs on the field but also illuminate the broader impact these players had on their communities and the sport itself.

Dive into the tales of Jackie Robinson, the pioneer who shattered racial barriers and became a symbol of equality and perseverance. Experience the Miracle on Grass with the 1980 US Olympic Baseball Team, an underdog squad that defied expectations and captured the hearts of a nation. Meet trailblazers like Jackie Mitchell, the first woman in baseball, and Joe Nuxhall, the youngest Major Leaguer, whose stories showcase courage and passion at a young age.

Follow the journeys of iconic figures such as Hank Aaron, the Home Run Hero, and Cal Ripken Jr., the Iron Man, whose legacies extend far beyond their remarkable achievements on the field. Explore the perfect game pitched by Don Larsen, a moment of baseball perfection that is etched in history. Discover the Little League phenomenon, Mo'ne Davis, whose trailblazing performances challenged stereotypes and inspired a generation.

From the iconic Babe Ruth to the humanitarian Roberto Clemente, these stories highlight the diverse facets of baseball, blending athleticism, courage, and the enduring spirit of the players. Join me on this adventure through time and discover the incredible stories that have shaped the game we love. Let the inspiring narratives within these pages kindle a lifelong love for baseball and a belief that, with dedication and passion, anyone can become a legend in their own right.

Breaking Barriers: Jackie Robinson

Early Years and Introduction to Baseball

Jackie Robinson's story begins in Cairo, Georgia, where he was born in 1919. The youngest of five children, Robinson grew up in a time of segregation and racial prejudice, which shaped his character and future achievements. His family moved to Pasadena, California, where Robinson attended John Muir High School. It was here that his athletic talents began to shine. Robinson became a four-sport athlete, excelling in football, basketball, track, and, of course, baseball. In high school, his athletic prowess was evident as he made the varsity teams in multiple sports and earned the nickname "Jackrabbit" for his speed, especially on the football field.

Robinson's talent in athletics continued to flourish at Pasadena Junior College. He was a standout athlete, particularly in football and track. In track, he won awards in the broad jump, now known as the long jump, showcasing his extraordinary athletic ability. Despite the racial challenges of the time, Robinson's skills could not be overlooked. His athletic journey then took him to the University of California, Los Angeles (UCLA), where he became the university's first student to win varsity letters in four sports: football, basketball, track, and baseball. At UCLA, Robinson's baseball skills were honed, but interestingly, it was not his standout sport at the time. He was more recognized for his abilities in football as a running back and in track and field.

While at UCLA, Robinson faced financial difficulties and had to leave school just shy of graduation. He moved to Honolulu, Hawaii, for a brief period to play semi-professional football with the Honolulu Bears. This experience was cut short by the onset of World War II. Robinson was drafted into the Army in 1942, where he faced racial discrimination and adversity, including a court-martial for refusing to move to the back of a segregated bus. He was acquitted of the charges and received an honorable discharge in 1944. This incident was a precursor to his later role in breaking the color barrier in professional baseball.

After his military service, Robinson briefly returned to athletic pursuits, playing basketball with the Los Angeles Red Devils. In 1945, his baseball career took a significant turn when he was signed to play for the Kansas City Monarchs in the Negro Leagues. His time with the Monarchs was marked by standout performances despite the challenging travel conditions and discrimination faced by players in the Negro Leagues. Robinson's career in the Negro Leagues was a stepping stone to his groundbreaking entry into Major League Baseball, setting the stage for his legendary role in breaking baseball's color barrier and paving the way for future generations of African American athletes.

Joining Major League Baseball

The year 1947 marked a pivotal moment in baseball and American history when Jackie Robinson shattered the color barrier in Major League Baseball. His signing with the Brooklyn Dodgers was not just a personal achievement but a monumental step in the civil rights movement. Branch Rickey, the Dodgers' General Manager, was determined to integrate baseball and saw Robinson as the ideal candidate to achieve this historic goal. Rickey knew that the player who would break baseball's color line had to be more than just a talented athlete; he needed the temperament and courage to withstand the inevitable racial hostility.

Robinson's debut on April 15, 1947, as a Brooklyn Dodger, was a highly anticipated and tense event. He faced enormous pressure, not only playing in the major leagues but also carrying the weight of hope and expectation from the African-American community and the scrutiny of a nation divided by racial attitudes. Despite this, Robinson's first season in the majors was nothing short of remarkable. He displayed exceptional skill and poise on the field, playing first base, a position he was not accustomed to. His performance earned him the inaugural Rookie of the Year award, which later was renamed in his honor.

Robinson's impact on the field was significant. His aggressive style of play, particularly his base-stealing ability, brought a new dynamism to the game. He was not just a skilled player but a catalyst for change in the way the game was played. Off the field, Robinson faced relentless racial abuse from fans and some fellow players. Despite this, he adhered to a promise he had made to Rickey to not retaliate for his first three years in the league. His dignity and restraint in the face of such adversity won him many admirers and helped slowly change attitudes among his teammates, opponents, and fans.

Robinson's first season was the beginning of a stellar career with the Dodgers that lasted a decade. He helped lead the team to six National League pennants and one World Series championship in 1955. Beyond his athletic achievements, Robinson's presence in Major League Baseball challenged and began to change deeply entrenched racial prejudices, both in baseball and in American society. His courage, resilience, and extraordinary skill paved the way for other African-American players and contributed significantly to the civil rights movement in the United States. Jackie Robinson's breaking of the color barrier in baseball is not just a sports milestone but a significant chapter in the story of America's struggle for racial equality.

Challenges and Triumphs

Jackie Robinson's entry into Major League Baseball was a monumental step in sports history, but it came with its fair share of challenges and triumphs. Robinson, as the first African-American player in the modern era of Major League Baseball, faced an onslaught of racial prejudice, both on and off the field. The vitriol he encountered was not just from the opposing teams' players and fans but sometimes from his own teammates and coaches. Despite this, Robinson's response to these challenges was marked by incredible fortitude and grace, setting a precedent for how to confront and rise above racial bigotry.

On the field, Robinson encountered pitchers who would deliberately throw at him, basemen who would try to injure him, and players who hurled racial slurs. The abuse was not limited to the playing field; he received death threats and faced discrimination in hotels and restaurants with the team. In one notable incident, Robinson was refused service at a gas station until he had changed out of his team uniform. These experiences, though harrowing, did not deter him. Instead, they fueled his determination to succeed and break down racial barriers in the sport.

Off the field, Robinson faced a similar barrage of racism. He and his family were subjected to threats and hostile treatment in their own community. Despite the fame and acclaim he achieved, Robinson was not immune to the racial segregation and discrimination prevalent in America at the time. However, he chose to confront these challenges not with bitterness but with a resolve to prove his worth and integrity through his actions and performance. He became an active and vocal participant in the civil rights movement, using his status to speak out against racial injustice and support integration efforts.

Robinson's triumphs in the face of these challenges were not just personal victories but milestones in the journey toward racial equality in America. His perseverance and success helped change the perception of African-American athletes and paved the way for future generations. His ability to endure and excel under immense pressure and hostility inspired not only other athletes but countless individuals facing their own battles against discrimination. Jackie Robinson's story of confronting and overcoming racial prejudice serves as a powerful example of strength, resilience, and the capacity for sports to catalyze social change.

Lasting Impact

Jackie Robinson's legacy extends far beyond the baseball diamond, positioning him as a pivotal figure in the civil rights movement and an enduring symbol of perseverance and equality. His groundbreaking role in integrating Major League Baseball served as a catalyst for change in American society, challenging and altering long-standing racial norms and prejudices. Robinson's impact was not only felt in the realm of sports, but it also resonated across the broader socio-political landscape, making him an icon of the struggle for racial equality.

After retiring from baseball in 1956, Robinson continued to use his platform to fight for civil rights and social justice. He was an outspoken advocate for African-American rights and was actively involved in several civil rights events. His involvement in the NAACP, including serving as the organization's board chairman, exemplified his commitment to the cause. Robinson also extended his influence into the business world, helping to establish the Freedom National Bank in Harlem, an institution aimed at supporting the African-American community. His forays into the business and civil rights arenas underscored his belief in economic empowerment as a path to racial equality.

Robinson's role in breaking baseball's color barrier had a ripple effect across other sports and areas of American life, paving the way for the integration of other professional sports leagues. His story inspired generations of athletes, both black and white, to pursue their dreams regardless of the obstacles they might face. Robinson's life and achievements became a blueprint for perseverance in the face of adversity, encouraging individuals to stand up for their rights and strive for excellence despite societal barriers.

Robinson's posthumous recognitions further cement his status as a civil rights pioneer and a hero. In 1997, Major League Baseball universally retired his jersey number, 42, across all teams - a unique honor that underscores his profound impact on the sport and society. Every year on April 15th, Jackie Robinson Day is celebrated in Major League Baseball, with players from every team wearing the number 42 in his honor, serving as a reminder of his enduring legacy. Through his unwavering courage, determination, and commitment to equality, Jackie Robinson's legacy continues to inspire and influence, making him not just a sports legend but a timeless symbol of resilience and the pursuit of justice.

The Miracle on Grass: 1980 US Olympic Baseball Team

Background and Team Formation

The story of the 1980 US Olympic Baseball Team, often referred to as "The Miracle on Grass," is a captivating tale of underdog triumph and national pride. This team's journey to the 1980 Olympics in Moscow was marked by unexpected challenges and extraordinary achievements. The squad was composed predominantly of amateur and collegiate players, a stark contrast to the professional, seasoned athletes they would face in the international arena. This unique mix of young talents from various universities and amateur clubs across the United States brought a fresh and dynamic approach to the team.

The formation of the 1980 Olympic team was a meticulous process, guided by the goal of assembling a group of players who could not only compete at an international level but also embody the spirit and determination of American baseball. The team's roster included promising college players, some of whom would later achieve significant success in Major League Baseball. This blend of youthful enthusiasm and raw talent was seen as both a strength and a vulnerability, as the team lacked the experience of playing together and facing international competition.

The team's preparation for the Olympics was an intensive period of training and team-building. Coaches focused on honing the skills of these young players, developing strategies that would leverage their strengths against the more experienced international teams. The players underwent rigorous training sessions, which included not only physical conditioning and skill development but also lessons on the nuances of international play, which differed in some respects from American baseball.

As the team came together, a sense of camaraderie and shared purpose began to develop among the players. Despite their diverse backgrounds and limited experience playing as a unit, they shared a common goal: to represent their country on the world stage and challenge the dominant international teams. This unity and determination would become the defining characteristics of the 1980 US Olympic Baseball Team, setting the stage for what would become one of the most remarkable stories in the history of Olympic baseball.

Underdog Status

The 1980 US Olympic Baseball Team's underdog status was a significant aspect of their narrative, particularly in the context of their competition against the Soviet Union team. The Soviet team, composed of seasoned and professionally trained athletes, was seen as a formidable opponent. They had the advantage of extensive experience in international play, a well-established baseball program, and were competing on their home turf, factors that contributed to their perception as the overwhelming favorites. In contrast, the US team, with its roster of amateur and collegiate players, lacked the depth of international experience and the kind of rigorous, specialized training that their Soviet counterparts had received.

This contrast in experience and preparation set the stage for what many viewed as a lopsided contest. The American team's relative inexperience in international competition and their youth were seen as major disadvantages. However, what the US team lacked in experience, they made up for with raw talent, enthusiasm, and a strong desire to prove themselves on the global stage. Their underdog status became a unifying force for the team, fueling their determination to defy expectations and make a mark in the Olympics.

The perception of the US team as underdogs was not just a reflection of their inexperience but also of the broader context of the Cold War. The political tensions between the United States and the Soviet Union added a layer of intensity to the competition, making the baseball field an extension of the larger geopolitical struggle. This backdrop added to the pressure on the young American team, as their performance was seen as more than just a sporting endeavor; it was a representation of national pride and resilience in the face of a powerful adversary.

Despite the odds stacked against them, the US team approached the competition with a positive mindset and a focus on teamwork and strategic play. Their underdog status allowed them to enter the tournament with a sense of freedom and a nothing-to-lose attitude, which proved to be advantageous. The team's journey through the tournament showcased their growing confidence and skill, challenging the preconceived notions of their capabilities and setting the stage for what would become a legendary performance in the annals of Olympic baseball.

Key Moments of the Game

The 1980 US Olympic Baseball Team's journey was marked by several key moments and pivotal plays that culminated in their unexpected victory, particularly in their games against the Soviet Union team. Each game was a tapestry of strategic plays, individual brilliance, and collective effort, with certain moments standing out as turning points in their path to victory. One such moment was a crucial home run hit by a relatively unknown player, which not only boosted the team's morale but also sent a clear message to their opponents about the American team's capability and resolve.

Another significant play was a masterful pitching performance by one of the team's starters. Against a backdrop of high pressure and expectations, this pitcher delivered an exceptional game, striking out several key players from the Soviet team. His performance not only silenced skeptics but also galvanized the American team, reinforcing their belief in their ability to compete against more experienced teams.

Defensive plays were equally pivotal in the US team's success. There were instances of remarkable fielding, including a game-saving catch in the outfield and a critical double play that thwarted a potential rally by the Soviet team. These defensive masterstrokes were not just displays of athletic prowess but also strategic triumphs, showcasing the team's ability to stay calm and focused under pressure.

The team's batting lineup also had its moments of brilliance, with several players contributing to key hits that drove in crucial runs. The collective effort of the team's batters, working in tandem to build pressure on the Soviet pitchers, demonstrated their strategic acumen and adaptability. These batting performances, particularly in clutch situations, were instrumental in swinging the momentum in favor of the American team.

The culmination of these key moments was not just in the individual plays but in how they came together to form a narrative of resilience, teamwork, and the triumph of the underdog. The US team's journey through these games was a series of challenges turned into opportunities, each play building on the last to create a story that resonated far beyond the baseball field. Their victory, achieved through a combination of skill, strategy, and sheer determination, became a defining moment in Olympic baseball history, leaving a lasting impression on all who witnessed it.

Significance of the Win

The victory of the 1980 US Olympic Baseball Team held profound significance not only for the sport of baseball but also for the Olympic Games and the nation as a whole. This win was more than just a triumph in a sports tournament; it represented a remarkable achievement against overwhelming odds and became a source of inspiration and national pride. The success of this young, inexperienced team in a global arena like the Olympics served as a powerful testament to the spirit of perseverance and the potential of teamwork.

In the realm of baseball, the team's victory was a defining moment that highlighted the depth of talent in American baseball, extending beyond the professional leagues. It demonstrated that with the right mix of skill, dedication, and leadership, even a team with less experience could achieve greatness on the world stage. This win contributed significantly to raising the profile of baseball in the Olympics, showcasing the sport's global appeal and competitiveness.

For the Olympic Games, the American team's success was a testament to the ethos of the Olympics – bringing together athletes from diverse backgrounds to compete on a level playing field. It reinforced the idea that the Olympics were not just about winning medals but also about celebrating the human spirit, sportsmanship, and the unifying power of sports. The US team's victory was a story of underdogs triumphing, a narrative that resonates deeply with the Olympic ideals.

Nationally, the victory came at a time when the United States needed a boost of morale. The team's unexpected success provided a sense of joy and pride to Americans, serving as a reminder of the country's resilience and capability. The players, with their diverse backgrounds and humble beginnings, represented the quintessential American spirit of hard work and determination. Their win was a source of inspiration for young athletes and non-athletes alike, demonstrating that with passion and perseverance, any challenge can be overcome and any dream can be achieved.

The legacy of this victory continued to inspire future generations of athletes and sports enthusiasts. The story of the 1980 US Olympic Baseball Team became a cherished part of American sports history, a narrative that spoke to the heart of what it means to strive against the odds, to work as a team, and to achieve something greater than the sum of individual efforts. This remarkable win left an indelible mark on the sports world, reminding everyone of the power of sports to unite, inspire, and celebrate human achievement.

The First Woman in Baseball: Jackie Mitchell

Early Life and Interest in Baseball

Jackie Mitchell's story, as the first woman in baseball, begins with her early life, which set the stage for her groundbreaking career. Born in 1913 in Chattanooga, Tennessee, Mitchell developed an interest in baseball at a very young age. This interest was not incidental; it was nurtured by her father, who was an avid baseball fan, and by a fortuitous neighborhood connection to a future Hall of Fame pitcher, Dazzy Vance. Vance, who lived nearby, noticed Mitchell's enthusiasm for the game and took it upon himself to teach her the art of pitching. Under his guidance, Mitchell honed her skills, particularly mastering the art of the curveball, a pitch that would later become her signature on the mound.

Mitchell's passion for baseball was not common for girls of her time, as the sport was predominantly male-dominated. However, her talent and determination were undeniable. She played for several local teams, often being the only girl on the team, and quickly made a name for herself with her pitching prowess. Her ability to play alongside and often outperform her male counterparts caught the attention of many, including Joe Engel, the president of the Chattanooga Lookouts, a minor-league baseball team.

Engel, known for his promotional stunts, saw potential in Mitchell's unique skill and her ability to draw crowds. In 1931, at the age of 17, Mitchell's baseball career took a significant turn when Engel signed her to a contract with the Chattanooga Lookouts. This signing was not only a personal achievement for Mitchell but also a historic moment for women in sports. It challenged the prevailing norms and perceptions about women's capabilities in professional sports, especially in a sport like baseball, which was then considered a bastion of masculinity.

Mitchell's early life and her gradual immersion into the world of baseball laid the groundwork for what would become a legendary moment in sports history. Her journey from playing in local teams to being signed by a professional team was marked by perseverance, skill, and a deep love for the game. This journey was not just about playing baseball; it was about challenging stereotypes and opening doors for future generations of women athletes. Jackie Mitchell's early life and interest in baseball were the first chapters of a story that would inspire countless girls and women to pursue their dreams in the face of societal constraints.

Signing with the Chattanooga Lookouts

Jackie Mitchell's signing with the Chattanooga Lookouts in 1931 was a landmark event in the history of baseball and sports at large. This momentous occasion shattered gender norms and redefined what was possible for women in the realm of professional sports. The Lookouts, a minor league team, were known for their willingness to experiment and push boundaries under the guidance of their president, Joe Engel, who was often referred to as the "P.T. Barnum of Baseball" due to his flair for showmanship and promotion. Engel's decision to sign Mitchell was partly driven by his knack for attracting public attention to his team, but it also spoke to Mitchell's undeniable skill as a pitcher.

Mitchell's contract with the Chattanooga Lookouts was not just a publicity stunt; it was a testament to her pitching ability, especially her exceptional curveball. Her signing attracted significant media attention, sparking debates and discussions about the role of women in professional sports. It challenged the deeply entrenched belief that baseball, a sport synonymous with American masculinity, was an exclusive domain for men. Her presence on the team was a bold statement against the gender barriers that existed in sports at the time.

The process of Mitchell being signed to the Lookouts involved not just recognition of her talent but also a willingness to confront and challenge the status quo. Engel, by signing Mitchell, demonstrated a progressive attitude towards gender roles in sports, providing an opportunity that was unprecedented for a woman in that era. This move was met with a mix of skepticism, curiosity, and admiration from the public and the baseball community.

Mitchell's signing with the Lookouts was more than just a personal achievement; it was a symbolic victory for women in sports. It paved the way for a broader conversation about women's participation in professional sports and set a precedent for challenging gender norms. Her presence on the team, even if short-lived, was a significant step in the journey toward gender equality in sports and served as an inspiration for future generations of female athletes. Jackie Mitchell's signing with a professional men's baseball team was a groundbreaking moment, not only in her career but in the annals of sports history, marking the beginning of a new chapter in the fight for gender equality in the athletic world.

Striking Out Babe Ruth and Lou Gehrig

The most legendary moment in Jackie Mitchell's career, and arguably one of the most remarkable in baseball history, occurred on April 2, 1931, when she faced two of the greatest baseball players of all time: Babe Ruth and Lou Gehrig. This event took place during an exhibition game between the Chattanooga Lookouts and the New York Yankees. Mitchell, then just 17 years old, stepped onto the mound with a calm demeanor that belied the monumental task ahead of her. The stage was set for what would become a defining moment in her career and a historic event in baseball.

When Babe Ruth approached the plate, the crowd buzzed with excitement and anticipation. Ruth, known as the "Sultan of Swat," was a towering figure in baseball, renowned for his home run-hitting prowess. Mitchell, undeterred by the challenge, wound up and delivered her pitches with precision. To the astonishment of the spectators, Ruth swung and missed at the first two pitches, both curveballs. The third pitch resulted in another swing and a miss, striking out one of baseball's greatest hitters. The crowd erupted in disbelief and admiration. Mitchell's successful strikeout of Babe Ruth was not just a personal triumph; it was a moment that shattered prevailing stereotypes about women in sports.

The excitement in the stadium escalated as Lou Gehrig, another legendary figure in baseball, stepped up to bat. Gehrig, known as the "Iron Horse," was celebrated for his hitting consistency and strength. However, Mitchell's skill on the mound was undiminished. She pitched with the same focus and control she had shown against Ruth. Gehrig, like Ruth, was unable to connect with Mitchell's curveballs and was quickly struck out. Striking out two of the most formidable batters back-to-back was an extraordinary feat, one that demonstrated Mitchell's remarkable talent and solidified her place in baseball folklore.

This game was more than just a sports competition; it was a cultural event that challenged the perceptions of women's abilities in traditionally male-dominated fields. Mitchell's striking out of Babe Ruth and Lou Gehrig was a statement of her skill, determination, and the potential for women to compete at the highest levels in sports. This moment resonated far beyond the baseball field, inspiring countless women and girls and becoming a symbol of breaking gender barriers. Jackie Mitchell's performance in this legendary game remains one of the most iconic moments in sports history, a testament to her extraordinary talent and the limitless potential of women in sports.

Legacy and Impact

Jackie Mitchell's impact on baseball and women's sports is profound and enduring. Her achievements, particularly striking out Babe Ruth and Lou Gehrig, transcended the baseball diamond and became a powerful symbol of women's capabilities in sports. Mitchell's career challenged the prevailing notions of gender roles in athletics during a time when women's participation in professional sports was largely unheard of and often discouraged. Her courage and skill in a male-dominated field paved the way for future generations of female athletes, inspiring them to pursue their dreams in sports and other areas traditionally dominated by men.

Mitchell's legacy is not just about her remarkable skill as a baseball player; it is also about the barriers she broke and the conversations she started. Her presence in professional baseball sparked discussions about women's roles in sports and helped to slowly shift public perception about women's capabilities in athletics. Although her career with the Chattanooga Lookouts was short-lived, the impact of her presence in the sport continued to resonate. Her story encouraged other women to take up sports, fostering a gradual change in the sports world that would lead to more opportunities for women athletes in the future.

Beyond her immediate impact on baseball, Mitchell's story is a part of the broader history of women's struggle for equality in all areas of life. Her journey in baseball mirrored the challenges faced by women in various fields, making her an icon of the larger fight for gender equality. Mitchell's achievements in a sport that was quintessentially American and traditionally male serve as a reminder of the importance of challenging stereotypes and breaking down gender barriers.

The legacy of Jackie Mitchell is a demonstration of the power of perseverance and the importance of challenging societal norms. Her story continues to inspire not just female athletes but anyone who faces obstacles in pursuit of their goals. Mitchell demonstrated that with talent, determination, and the courage to defy conventions, it is possible to overcome seemingly insurmountable barriers. Her place in sports history serves as an enduring reminder of what can be achieved when we refuse to be limited by the expectations of society and dare to pursue our passions, regardless of gender.

Youngest Major Leaguer: Joe Nuxhall

Early Interest in Baseball

Joe Nuxhall's journey to becoming the youngest player ever in Major League Baseball began with a deep-rooted passion for the game that was evident from his early childhood. Born in Hamilton, Ohio, in 1928, Nuxhall grew up in a family where baseball was a cherished pastime. His father, Orville Nuxhall, played a pivotal role in nurturing his son's love for the game, often playing catch with him and teaching him the fundamentals of pitching. This early exposure to baseball laid the foundation for Nuxhall's future in the sport.

From a young age, Nuxhall showed a natural talent for baseball, particularly pitching. He honed his skills playing for local youth teams in Hamilton, where his exceptional arm strength and pitching ability quickly became apparent. His talent on the mound was complemented by his height and physical stature, which made him stand out among his peers. Nuxhall's dedication to the game was evident in his commitment to practice and his desire to constantly improve his skills.

Nuxhall's early baseball experiences were not just about developing his talent; they were also about fostering his love for the game. He spent countless hours on local fields, playing in various youth leagues and pick-up games, often competing against older and more experienced players. These experiences were crucial in building his confidence and preparing him for the challenges of professional baseball. Nuxhall's passion for baseball was more than just a hobby; it was a driving force that would eventually lead him to an extraordinary opportunity in Major League Baseball at an incredibly young age.

This early phase of Nuxhall's life, filled with baseball games, practice sessions, and a growing mastery of pitching, was the beginning of a remarkable journey. His early years in baseball were marked by a combination of natural talent, a supportive family environment, and an unwavering passion for the game. These elements came together to create the foundation for Nuxhall's historic entry into Major League Baseball, setting the stage for his record-breaking debut as the youngest player in the history of the league.

Debut at 15

Joe Nuxhall's debut in Major League Baseball (MLB) at the age of 15 is a story of extraordinary circumstances and a testament to his remarkable talent as a young pitcher. The backdrop of World War II played a crucial role in this unusual event. In 1944, as many of the MLB's established players were serving in the military, teams were in dire need of new talent to fill their rosters. This need opened an unexpected door for Nuxhall, whose abilities had caught the attention of scouts despite his young age.

The Cincinnati Reds, Nuxhall's hometown team, were among those searching for new players. Bill McKechnie, the manager of the Reds at the time, and their scouts saw potential in the young Nuxhall. They were impressed by his physical stature, which was unusually mature for his age, and his impressive pitching skills. Recognizing the unique opportunity to bring a local talent into the big leagues, the Reds decided to take a chance on Nuxhall, offering him a contract. This decision was both a nod to Nuxhall's potential and a reflection of the extraordinary circumstances of the time.

Nuxhall's MLB debut on June 10, 1944, was as much a surprise to him as it was to the world of baseball. At the tender age of 15 years and 10 months, he took the mound for the Reds against the St. Louis Cardinals. The game was a significant challenge for Nuxhall, who faced some of the best hitters in the league with limited experience. His debut was a mixture of excitement, nerves, and the raw talent of a young athlete thrust into the spotlight. Although his initial appearance was brief and marked by the expected struggles of a young, inexperienced player, it was a historic moment in MLB history.

Nuxhall's debut at such a young age was not just a novelty; it was a moment that spoke to the potential of young athletes and the importance of nurturing talent. His first foray into the major leagues was the beginning of a long and successful career in baseball. This extraordinary start was a defining moment in Nuxhall's life, setting him on a path that would see him return to the Reds and establish himself as a significant figure in the team's history. His debut at 15 remains one of the most fascinating and inspiring stories in the history of baseball, showcasing the unexpected opportunities that can arise and the remarkable potential of young talent.

Challenges and Growth

Joe Nuxhall's entry into Major League Baseball at the age of 15 presented him with an array of challenges, particularly competing against seasoned professionals. His debut game, while historic, highlighted the stark difference in experience between the young Nuxhall and veteran players. Facing batters who had years of professional baseball under their belts, Nuxhall struggled to find his footing in his first outing. He experienced the typical difficulties of any young player, such as controlling his nerves, managing the mental aspects of the game, and handling the physical demands of playing at a higher level.

After his initial exposure to the major leagues, Nuxhall returned to the minor leagues to further develop his skills. This period was fundamental for his growth both as a pitcher and as a person. In the minors, he had the opportunity to refine his pitching techniques, build his physical strength, and gain much-needed experience against a variety of hitters. These years in the minors were instrumental in Nuxhall's development, providing him with a platform to mature and improve away from the intense scrutiny of the major leagues.

During his time in the minor leagues, Nuxhall faced the challenge of balancing his baseball career with his education and personal life. Being thrust into professional baseball at such a young age meant that he had to navigate the complexities of adulthood while still in his teenage years. He had to learn how to manage his time effectively, cope with the pressures of professional sports, and maintain his commitment to his personal growth.

Nuxhall's journey back to the major leagues was marked by persistence and determination. He worked tirelessly to improve his game, learning from each experience and using setbacks as opportunities for growth. His return to the Cincinnati Reds in the early 1950s was a reflection of his hard work and development as a player. This comeback marked the beginning of a successful career in the majors, where Nuxhall established himself as a reliable and skilled pitcher. His ability to overcome the initial challenges and grow into a mature and accomplished player is a significant part of his legacy, showcasing the importance of resilience and continuous improvement in the face of adversity.

Legacy and Career After the Debut

Joe Nuxhall's legacy in baseball extends far beyond his record as the youngest player to appear in a Major League game. After his return to the majors, Nuxhall established himself as a reliable and skilled pitcher for the Cincinnati Reds. Over his career, he became known for his left-handed pitching, recording impressive stats that included multiple All-Star game appearances. His playing career, spanning more than 15 years, was marked by consistent performance and sportsmanship, earning him respect and admiration from teammates, opponents, and fans alike.

Beyond his achievements on the mound, Nuxhall's contribution to baseball continued after his playing days were over. He transitioned into a broadcasting career, becoming a beloved radio voice for the Cincinnati Reds. His deep knowledge of the game, combined with his engaging storytelling ability, made him a favorite among Reds fans. For over three decades, Nuxhall narrated games with a unique blend of expertise and enthusiasm, endearing him to a new generation of baseball enthusiasts.

Nuxhall's commitment to the community was another significant aspect of his legacy. He was actively involved in charitable work, particularly in his hometown of Hamilton, Ohio. His contributions to youth sports programs and various community initiatives reflected his dedication to giving back and supporting the growth of baseball at the grassroots level. This community involvement further cemented his status as a beloved figure in Cincinnati and beyond.

Joe Nuxhall's legacy is not only measured by his record-breaking debut and his achievements as a player but also by his impact as a broadcaster and community figure. His life and career in baseball demonstrate the importance of adaptability, passion for the game, and commitment to the community. Nuxhall remains a cherished figure in the history of the Cincinnati Reds and Major League Baseball, embodying the spirit of perseverance and the love of the game. His journey from a 15-year-old rookie to a respected veteran and broadcaster is a compelling narrative of growth, dedication, and lasting impact on the sport he loved.

The Home Run Hero: Hank Aaron

Early Life and Start in Baseball

Hank Aaron's journey to becoming one of the greatest baseball players of all time began with a humble upbringing and a profound love for the game. Born in 1934 in Mobile, Alabama, Aaron grew up in a poor family during the era of racial segregation in the South. His early life was marked by challenges, but it was also in these formative years that Aaron developed a passion for baseball, a sport that would later become his life's calling.

As a young boy, Aaron found creative ways to play baseball despite the lack of resources. He would make his own bats and balls from materials he found, demonstrating his determination to pursue his passion for the game. This ingenuity and love for baseball were evident from an early age, setting the stage for his future success. Aaron's family, particularly his brother Tommie

Aaron, who also became a Major League Baseball player, played a significant role in his early interest in the sport.

Aaron's talent in baseball became apparent during his years at Central High School and Josephine Allen Institute, a private school in Mobile. However, due to the racial barriers of the time, his opportunities to play organized baseball were limited. This did not deter Aaron; he played in semi-professional and amateur teams, showcasing his burgeoning skills. His performance on these teams caught the attention of scouts from the Negro Leagues.

In 1951, at the age of 17, Aaron began his professional baseball career with the Indianapolis Clowns of the Negro Leagues. His time in the Negro Leagues was brief but significant, as it provided him with the opportunity to play against some of the best African American players of the era. Aaron's exceptional talent was evident in his performance with the Clowns, where he played shortstop and outfield. His stint in the Negro Leagues was a critical stepping stone, leading to his signing by the Boston Braves, who later became the Atlanta Braves, in Major League Baseball.

Aaron's early life and start in baseball were characterized by his resilience, determination, and undeniable talent. His journey from playing with homemade equipment in the streets of Mobile to starring in the Negro Leagues and eventually making his mark in Major League Baseball is a reflection of his perseverance and passion for the game. Aaron's humble beginnings and rise through the ranks of professional baseball serve as an inspiring story of overcoming obstacles and achieving greatness.

Chase for the Record

Hank Aaron's pursuit of Babe Ruth's longstanding home run record is one of the most captivating chapters in baseball history.

This quest, marked by determination and resilience, began to take shape as Aaron's talent for hitting home runs became increasingly evident in his early years with the Braves. Ruth's record of 714 home runs had stood as a seemingly unassailable benchmark for decades, and the thought of it being broken was almost unimaginable to many baseball fans. However, Aaron's consistent power-hitting placed him on a path to challenge this legendary record.

Throughout the 1950s and 1960s, Aaron established himself as one of the best hitters in baseball, steadily accumulating home runs each season. His approach at the plate was a blend of impeccable timing, raw power, and a keen eye for the ball, making him one of the most feared hitters in the league. Season after season, Aaron's home run tally grew, and the possibility of surpassing Ruth's record began to seem not just a distant dream but an achievable goal.

One of the key milestones in Aaron's chase was the 1973 season. He finished the season with 713 home runs, just one short of tying Ruth's record. The anticipation and excitement were palpable as the 1974 season approached, with fans and media closely watching Aaron's every at-bat. The pressure and expectations were immense, but Aaron handled them with grace and focus, demonstrating not just his physical skill but also his mental fortitude.

On April 8, 1974, in front of a packed stadium in Atlanta and millions of viewers on television, Aaron made history. In the fourth inning against the Los Angeles Dodgers, he hit his 715th career home run, breaking Babe Ruth's record. This historic home run was more than just a personal achievement for Aaron; it was a monumental moment in the sport's history. The image of Aaron rounding the bases, with fans cheering and fireworks lighting up the sky, remains one of the most iconic in baseball.

Aaron's pursuit and eventual breaking of Babe Ruth's home run record was a journey filled with challenges, milestones, and unforgettable moments. It was a testament to his enduring talent, consistency, and resilience. This remarkable feat not only solidified Aaron's place in baseball lore but also resonated beyond the sport, symbolizing the triumph of skill and perseverance over daunting obstacles. His chase for the record is remembered not just for the record itself but for the way Aaron carried himself throughout the journey, with dignity and integrity in the face of immense pressure and scrutiny.

Overcoming Racism and Adversity

As Hank Aaron approached Babe Ruth's historic home run record, he faced not only the pressure of the chase but also the harsh reality of racism and adversity. During this period, Aaron found himself at the center of a racially charged environment, reflective of the broader social tensions in America at the time. His pursuit of one of baseball's most sacred records brought him under an intense and often hostile spotlight, with racial abuse becoming a disturbing part of his daily experience.

The closer Aaron got to breaking Ruth's record, the more intense the racial backlash became. He received a torrent of hate mail and death threats, many of which were explicitly racist in nature. These threats were not just directed at Aaron but also at his family, creating a constant state of fear and concern for their safety. The Federal Bureau of Investigation (FBI) got involved, monitoring the threats and ensuring Aaron's security. Despite this protective measure, the emotional and psychological impact on Aaron was significant. He had to endure the hatred and bigotry directed at him, simply for excelling in the sport he loved.

Amidst this torrent of racism, Aaron demonstrated remarkable strength and resilience. He refused to let the hate and threats deter him from his goal. His ability to maintain his focus and performance on the field, despite the off-field turmoil, was a demonstration of his mental fortitude. Aaron's demeanor during this time was one of quiet dignity and grace under pressure. He became an unwitting symbol of the struggle against racism, using his platform and performance to make a statement against the discrimination and hatred he faced.

Aaron's experience while chasing Ruth's record highlighted the persistent issue of racism in sports and society. His struggle against this adversity was not just about a baseball record; it was emblematic of the broader fight for equality and respect for African-American athletes. The challenges Aaron faced and overcame during this period added a layer of significance to his eventual record-breaking achievement. His triumph over racism and adversity became an inspiring chapter in his legacy, demonstrating the power of perseverance and the human spirit in the face of hatred and discrimination. Aaron's journey through this tumultuous time left an indelible mark on the history of baseball and the ongoing fight for racial equality.

Legacy Beyond Home Runs

Hank Aaron's legacy extends far beyond his monumental home run record. His career in Major League Baseball is marked by a plethora of achievements and contributions that solidified his status as one of the greatest players in the sport's history. Aaron's prowess on the baseball field was not limited to home runs; he was also known for his exceptional hitting ability, resulting in a career batting average of over .300, numerous All-Star game appearances, and multiple Gold Glove awards for his defensive skills. His consistency and longevity in the game were remarkable, demonstrated by his record for the most career runs batted in (RBI), evidence of his role as a dependable and formidable player for his team.

Beyond his athletic achievements, Aaron's impact as a civil rights advocate and mentor is a significant part of his legacy. He used his platform as a renowned athlete to speak out against racism and advocate for equality, both within baseball and in wider society. His own experiences with racial discrimination fueled his commitment to civil rights and social justice issues. Aaron was actively involved in various philanthropic endeavors, focusing particularly on empowering African-American youth. He established the Hank Aaron Chasing the Dream Foundation to provide scholarships and support for young people pursuing their dreams.

Aaron's role as a mentor and advocate for young players, especially African-American athletes, was a hallmark of his post-playing career. He was instrumental in guiding and inspiring the next generation of players, sharing his knowledge, experience, and wisdom. His efforts to promote diversity in baseball, both on the field and in front-office positions, reflected his dedication to breaking down racial barriers and fostering inclusivity in the sport.

Hank Aaron's legacy is multifaceted, encompassing his extraordinary contributions to baseball, his advocacy for civil rights, and his commitment to mentoring and supporting the next generation. His life and career serve as an inspiring example of excellence, resilience, and social responsibility. Aaron's impact on baseball and society resonates far beyond his home run record, making him a revered figure not only in the world of sports but also as a champion for equality and positive change. His legacy continues to inspire and influence, reminding us of the power of sports as a platform for social progress and the importance of using one's voice and talents to make a difference in the world.

The Perfect Game: Don Larsen

Background and Early Career

Don Larsen's journey to pitching the only perfect game in World Series history is a story of resilience and unexpected triumph. Born in 1929 in Michigan City, Indiana, Larsen's early life was marked by a love for baseball. Growing up, he honed his skills in the game, leading to his eventual entry into professional baseball. His early career, however, was not a straightforward path to success. It was characterized by challenges and learning experiences that shaped him into the player capable of achieving one of the most remarkable feats in baseball history.

Larsen began his Major League Baseball career with the St. Louis Browns in 1953. His initial years in the majors were a period of adjustment and development. As a starting pitcher, Larsen showed potential, but his performance was inconsistent. He struggled with control, often battling with his pitch accuracy, which led to a less-than-stellar start to his career. His time with the Browns, and later with the Baltimore Orioles after the Browns relocated and became the Orioles, was a learning curve, providing him with valuable experience in the major leagues.

In 1954, Larsen's career took a significant turn when he was traded to the New York Yankees. This move to one of the most storied franchises in baseball presented Larsen with a new set of opportunities and challenges. With the Yankees, he found himself in a highly competitive environment, surrounded by some of the game's best players. This change of scenery and the higher stakes of playing for a perennial championship-contending team pushed Larsen to refine his skills and adapt to the pressures of playing for a high-profile team.

During his early years with the Yankees, Larsen continued to work on improving his pitching. He was known for his powerful right arm and a wide range of pitches, but consistency remained an issue. Despite these struggles, Larsen's potential was evident and he became a valuable member of the Yankees' pitching staff. His journey through the early stages of his career, marked by ups and downs, set the stage for his historic performance in the 1956 World Series. Larsen's background and early career reflect the importance of perseverance and continuous improvement in professional sports, laying the foundation for his extraordinary achievement in the World Series.

The 1956 World Series

The 1956 World Series was a pivotal event in baseball history, featuring a matchup between the New York Yankees and the Brooklyn Dodgers. This series was set against the backdrop of a fierce rivalry, as the Yankees and Dodgers were two of the most dominant and celebrated teams of the era. The Yankees, with their storied history and multiple World Series titles, were seen as the epitome of baseball success. The Dodgers, on the other hand, were a powerhouse in their own right, having won the World Series the previous year in 1955.

The significance of the 1956 World Series extended beyond the rivalry. It was a clash of baseball titans, with both teams boasting rosters filled with legendary players. The Yankees, led by the likes of Mickey Mantle, Yogi Berra, and Whitey Ford, were a formidable force, known for their powerful hitting and strong pitching. The Dodgers, featuring stars like Jackie Robinson, Duke Snider, and Roy Campanella, were equally impressive, known for their skillful play and strategic prowess.

The atmosphere surrounding the 1956 World Series was electric, with fans and media eagerly anticipating the games. The series was not just a sporting event; it was a cultural spectacle that captured the attention of the nation. Baseball fans were treated to a display of some of the best talents in the game, and the series promised to be a showcase of high-level baseball.

For the New York Yankees, the 1956 World Series was an opportunity to reclaim their title as the champions of baseball. After losing to the Dodgers in the 1955 World Series, the Yankees were determined to make a strong comeback. The team was under pressure to perform and live up to its reputation as one of the most successful franchises in sports history. This context set the stage for what would become one of the most memorable World Series in baseball history, with Don Larsen's perfect game adding an extraordinary chapter to the storied rivalry between the Yankees and the Dodgers.

The Perfect Game

Don Larsen's perfect game in Game 5 of the 1956 World Series against the Brooklyn Dodgers stands as one of the most remarkable achievements in baseball history. On October 8, 1956, at Yankee Stadium, Larsen accomplished what no other pitcher had done in World Series history — pitching a perfect game, a game with no hits, walks, or errors, and retiring all 27 batters he faced. The significance of this feat was magnified by the high-stakes atmosphere of the World Series and the formidable opponent he was facing in the Dodgers.

From the first pitch, Larsen exhibited exceptional control and composure on the mound. He efficiently worked through the Dodgers' lineup, known for its offensive prowess. His pitches were a blend of speed and accuracy, keeping the Dodgers' hitters off balance throughout the game. As the innings progressed, the tension and excitement in Yankee Stadium grew. Fans and players alike began to realize the historical significance of what was unfolding.

One of the key moments in the game came in the second inning when Jackie Robinson hit a line drive that seemed destined to be a hit. However, Yankee third baseman Andy Carey made a spectacular catch, preserving the perfect game. This play was emblematic of the razor-thin margin that often accompanies such a rare feat in baseball. As the game continued, Larsen remained unflappable, retiring batter after batter with a remarkable mix of pitches.

The final inning of the game was a pinnacle of suspense and excitement. With the stadium's atmosphere charged with anticipation, Larsen faced the last three Dodgers batters. Each out brought him closer to history. The final out, a called strikeout against Dale Mitchell, was met with an eruption of joy and disbelief from the crowd and Larsen's teammates. Catcher Yogi Berra famously leaped into Larsen's arms in a moment that has become one of the most iconic in baseball history.

Larsen's perfect game was a masterful performance, showcasing not just his skill as a pitcher but also his mental toughness. The pressure of maintaining a perfect game in such a high-stakes environment was immense, yet Larsen handled it with remarkable calmness and precision. This game was more than just a personal achievement for Larsen; it was a historic moment for baseball, a display of pitching excellence that has stood the test of time. The memory of Larsen's perfect game continues to be celebrated as one of the greatest moments in the history of the sport, a testament to the rare combination of skill, concentration, and a bit of baseball magic.

Legacy and Significance

The rarity and monumental difficulty of pitching a perfect game, especially in the context of the World Series, cannot be overstated. Don Larsen's perfect game in the 1956 World Series against the Brooklyn Dodgers remains one of the most extraordinary achievements in baseball history. This feat has a special place in the annals of the sport, not only because of its occurrence in the high-pressure environment of the World Series but also due to the sheer statistical improbability of its occurrence. A perfect game, defined as a game in which a pitcher (or combination of pitchers) allows no opposing player to reach base, is a rare event in baseball. Achieving this in the regular season is remarkable in itself, but accomplishing it during the World Series elevates it to a legendary status.

The significance of Larsen's perfect game extends beyond the record books. It has become a symbol of pitching excellence and a benchmark for all pitchers in the sport. The game has been recounted in countless baseball documentaries, books, and articles, often cited as one of the greatest moments in sports history. Larsen's achievement also brought a new level of fame and recognition to his career, which was otherwise characterized by its ups and downs. His perfect game transformed him from a relatively unknown pitcher into a household name, forever etching his name in baseball lore.

For the New York Yankees, Larsen's perfect game was a key moment in their storied history. It highlighted the team's dominance in the sport during that era and added another illustrious chapter to their legacy. For baseball fans, the game stands as a demonstration of the unpredictable and magical nature of the sport, where history can be made at any given moment. The game is a reminder of the beauty of baseball, where individual brilliance can shine brightly on the world's biggest stage.

Larsen's perfect game has also served as an inspiration to pitchers and players across generations. It is a reminder of what is possible on the baseball field and an example of achieving perfection under pressure. The legacy of Don Larsen's perfect game in the 1956 World Series endures as one of the most remarkable achievements in sports, a feat that continues to captivate and inspire the baseball world. The rarity and difficulty of what Larsen accomplished that day have ensured that his name will forever be remembered in the history of baseball as a symbol of excellence and a moment of perfection.

The Little League Phenomenon: Mo'ne Davis

Early Life and Love for Baseball

Mo'ne Davis' journey to becoming a Little League phenomenon and a symbol of breaking gender barriers in sports began with her early life in Philadelphia, Pennsylvania. Born in 2001, Davis was raised in a supportive environment where her athletic talents were nurtured from a young age. Her introduction to baseball came at the age of seven when she started playing in the Marian Anderson Recreation Center league. This early experience in a local league laid the foundation for her future success in the sport.

Davis' passion for baseball was evident from the outset. She was drawn to the game's complexity, the skills it demanded, and the teamwork it involved. Her natural talent was quickly recognized by her coaches, who admired her strong arm and her ability to play multiple positions with ease. Davis initially played various positions but soon found her calling as a pitcher, where her skills truly shone. Her ability to pitch with power and accuracy at a young age set her apart from her peers.

In addition to her talent on the field, Davis' early life in baseball was also shaped by her determination and work ethic. She was known for her dedication to practice, often spending extra hours honing her skills and understanding of the game. This commitment to excellence was coupled with a competitive spirit that drove her to excel in a sport predominantly played by boys.

Davis' early influences in baseball were not limited to her local league experiences. She looked up to and drew inspiration from various baseball players, both male and female, who had made their mark in the sport. These role models played a significant role in shaping her aspirations and approach to the game. Her early life in baseball, marked by her love for the game, her exceptional talent, and her inspiring work ethic, was the beginning of a journey that would lead her to national prominence and make her an icon for young athletes, especially girls aspiring to break into male-dominated sports.

Making History in Little League

Mo'ne Davis' journey to the Little League World Series (LLWS) is a groundbreaking chapter in the history of baseball, marked by her extraordinary achievements as a female pitcher. Her path to the LLWS began with her standout performances in local and regional Little League games. Playing for the Taney Dragons, a team based in Philadelphia, Davis quickly gained attention for her pitching prowess. Her ability to throw fastballs at speeds exceeding 70 miles per hour (113 kilometers per hour), coupled with her skillful use of off-speed pitches, set her apart in a sport predominantly played by boys.

In 2014, Davis' talent and hard work culminated in her leading the Taney Dragons to the Mid-Atlantic Regional Championship, securing their spot in the LLWS. This achievement was significant not only for Davis and her team but also for the broader context of women in baseball. Davis became one of the few girls to ever play in the LLWS, a tournament that has been a launching pad for many professional baseball players. Her participation in this prestigious event was a milestone for gender equality in sports.

At the LLWS, Davis' performance was nothing short of sensational. She captured the national spotlight with her remarkable pitching. In her first game, she pitched a shutout against a team from Nashville, Tennessee, striking out eight batters and allowing only two hits. This performance made her the first girl in LLWS history to pitch a winning game and the first to pitch a shutout. The game was a defining moment, not just in the tournament, but in the narrative of women's sports.

The significance of Davis' achievements in the LLWS extends beyond the statistics and the records she set. Her success on a global stage challenged long-standing stereotypes about the roles and capabilities of female athletes in male-dominated sports. Davis became a role model and an inspiration for countless young girls and boys, showing that talent and hard work can break down barriers. Her presence and success in the LLWS brought increased attention to women's participation in baseball and sparked conversations about gender inclusivity in sports. Mo'ne Davis' journey in the Little League World Series is a reflection of her skill, determination, and the changing landscape of sports, where gender barriers are continually being challenged and redefined.

Impactful Performances

Mo'ne Davis' performances in the 2014 Little League World Series (LLWS) were not just exceptional; they were historic and game-changing. Her standout performance, particularly her shutout game, is etched in the annals of the tournament as one of the most impressive displays of pitching prowess. In this game, Davis faced the team from Nashville, Tennessee, and showcased her extraordinary skills on the mound. Her fastball, clocked at speeds that rivaled those of her male counterparts, left batters struggling to connect. But it wasn't just the speed that was impressive; it was her control and the variety of her pitches that truly set her apart.

Davis pitched six innings in the shutout game, demonstrating stamina and focus that belied her age. She struck out eight batters, showcasing not just power but also strategic thinking in her pitch selection and placement. Her curveball and slider were particularly effective, leaving batters swinging and missing. This performance catapulted her into the national spotlight, drawing praise from baseball fans, professional players, and sports commentators alike.

The significance of her shutout game in the LLWS extended beyond the numbers on the scoreboard. It broke gender barriers, challenging the stereotypes about girls' participation in baseball. Davis became an overnight sensation, with her jersey being sent to the Baseball Hall of Fame, a testament to the historical importance of her achievement. Her poise and composure during the game, under the intense pressure of a national audience, spoke volumes about her character and her potential as a future athlete.

Moreover, Davis' performances in the LLWS were inspirational, not only to young girls who saw her as a role model but also to boys and coaches, who were reminded of the importance of inclusivity in sports. Her games were watched by millions, sparking conversations about women in baseball and the need for greater opportunities for girls in sports. Mo'ne Davis' standout performances in the LLWS, especially her shutout game, were more than just exceptional athletic feats; they were pivotal moments in the ongoing journey toward gender equality in sports.

Influence and Role Model

Mo'ne Davis' success in the Little League World Series had a profound impact on challenging gender stereotypes in sports, positioning her as a role model for young athletes, regardless of gender. Her achievements on the baseball field demonstrated that skill and talent do not conform to traditional gender norms. As a girl excelling in a sport predominantly played by boys, Davis shattered the stereotype that baseball is a male-only sport. Her presence and performance in the LLWS sent a powerful message about equality and inclusivity in sports.

Davis' role as a model for young girls is particularly significant. She showed that girls could compete at the highest levels in sports traditionally dominated by boys. Her success encourages more girls to take up baseball and other sports where female participation is less common. Parents, coaches, and organizations are inspired to support and provide more opportunities for girls in sports, acknowledging the importance of fostering an inclusive environment where talent can thrive irrespective of gender.

Moreover, Davis' influence extends to young boys and the broader sports community. Her skills and achievements earned her respect and admiration from her male peers, helping to break down gender biases among young athletes. Coaches and sports organizations are reminded of the importance of nurturing talent in all its forms, leading to a greater emphasis on equality in youth sports programs.

Davis became a national icon, not just for her athletic prowess but also for her poise, humility, and sportsmanship. She handled the intense media attention and the pressure of national exposure with maturity, becoming a positive influence for young athletes learning to balance sports with other aspects of their lives. Her story was not just about baseball; it was about perseverance, dedication, and breaking down barriers. Mo'ne Davis' success and her role as a model transcend sports, making her a symbol of progress in the ongoing pursuit of gender equality in all areas of life. Her influence as a role model continues to inspire the next generation of athletes, paving the way for a more inclusive and equitable sporting world.

The Iron Man: Cal Ripken Jr.

Early Career and Development

Cal Ripken Jr.'s journey to becoming "The Iron Man" of baseball, renowned for his record-breaking consecutive games played streak, began with his early years steeped in a family deeply rooted in baseball. Born in 1960 in Maryland, Ripken was raised in a household where baseball was a way of life. His father, Cal Ripken Sr., was deeply involved in the sport, working as a coach and manager in the Baltimore Orioles organization for many years. This environment profoundly influenced Ripken Jr., instilling in him a love for the game from a very young age.

Ripken's early exposure to baseball was comprehensive, encompassing every aspect of the game. He spent countless hours at ballparks, absorbing the nuances of baseball from his father and other players. This immersive experience was instrumental in shaping his understanding and approach to the game. Ripken didn't just learn the skills required to play baseball; he also absorbed the work ethic, discipline, and mental approach needed to excel in the sport.

Ripken's entry into Major League Baseball (MLB) was almost predestined given his upbringing. He was drafted by the Baltimore Orioles, the same organization his father served, in the second round of the 1978 MLB draft. This selection was the beginning of a long and illustrious career with the Orioles, a rarity in an era where players frequently moved between teams. Ripken quickly moved through the Orioles' minor league system, showcasing his potential as a versatile and skilled player.

In the early stages of his MLB career, Ripken made a significant impact with his consistent performance, versatility on the field, and ability to play multiple positions. He settled into the role of a shortstop, redefining the position traditionally reserved for smaller, more agile players. Ripken brought a combination of size, power, and defensive skills to the position, challenging the conventional mold of a shortstop. His early career was marked by rapid development, setting the stage for his emergence as one of the most durable and dependable players in the history of baseball. Ripken's early years in baseball laid a solid foundation for his legendary status as "The Iron Man," reflecting his deep-rooted connection to the sport and his commitment to excellence.

The Streak Begins

Cal Ripken Jr.'s consecutive games streak, a monumental record in the annals of baseball, began quite unassumingly on May 30, 1982. This date marked the beginning of what would become one of the most celebrated records in sports history. Ripken's streak was not initially intended as a pursuit of any record; rather, it started as a demonstration of his commitment to the game, his resilience, and his desire to contribute consistently to his team, the Baltimore Orioles.

During the early phase of the streak, Ripken established himself as a reliable and indispensable player for the Orioles. His ability to play day in and day out, without succumbing to the physical and mental fatigue that comes with the grueling MLB schedule, was extraordinary. Ripken's dedication to being a constant presence in the lineup showcased his remarkable physical fitness and his mental toughness.

The significance of the streak in the context of Ripken's career and the broader baseball world became more pronounced as the numbers started to accumulate. Playing every game, season after season, Ripken became the embodiment of durability in a sport where injuries and days off are commonplace. His streak was a throwback to the old-school ethos of baseball, where players often played through pain and fatigue.

As Ripken continued to play game after game, his streak began to attract national attention. It wasn't just about the number of games played; it was about the consistent level of performance that Ripken maintained throughout. He wasn't just showing up; he was contributing significantly to his team, both offensively and defensively. The streak started to be recognized not just as a numerical achievement but as a symbol of steadfast dedication and a deep love for the game of baseball.

In the era in which Ripken played, the streak became a remarkable feat, contrasting with the growing trend of player management and rest in professional sports. As the streak progressed, it became a part of Ripken's identity and a defining feature of his illustrious career. Each game added to the streak was a new chapter in a growing legacy, a testament to Ripken's enduring commitment to the game he loved. The beginning of Ripken's consecutive games streak was more than just the start of a record; it was the commencement of a legendary journey in baseball history.

Challenges and Perseverance

Maintaining a consecutive games streak as long as Cal Ripken Jr.'s in Major League Baseball posed numerous physical and mental challenges. The demands of playing day in and day out, through the lengthy and often grueling MLB season, were immense. For Ripken, this meant not only being physically present in each game but also maintaining a high level of performance, a challenge that required an extraordinary level of physical fitness, endurance, and mental resilience.

Physically, the streak demanded Ripken to be in peak condition year-round. He had to navigate the risk of injuries, fatigue, and the wear and tear that naturally comes with the intensity of professional baseball. Playing through minor injuries and managing physical discomfort became part of Ripken's routine. His approach to physical fitness and self-care was meticulous. He invested time in conditioning, recovery, and maintaining his health, understanding that his physical well-being was crucial to the continuation of the streak.

Mentally, the streak presented its own set of challenges. The pressure of keeping the streak alive, coupled with the expectations to perform well, could have been overwhelming. Ripken, however, managed these mental pressures with remarkable composure. His mental toughness and focus were as integral to his success as his physical abilities. He approached each game with the same level of commitment and intensity, regardless of external pressures or the personal significance of the streak.

Ripken's ability to consistently perform at a high level throughout the streak underscored his exemplary approach to the game. He maintained a strong work ethic, a deep understanding of baseball, and a strategic approach to both offense and defense. Ripken's dedication to honing his skills and adapting his play style as needed played a fundamental role in his ability to contribute effectively to his team in each game.

The challenges of maintaining such a lengthy streak were multifaceted, but Ripken's consistent performance, resilience in the face of adversity, and unwavering dedication to the sport were key to his success. The streak was more than just a display of physical endurance; it was a demonstration of Ripken's perseverance, mental strength, and unyielding passion for baseball. His approach to overcoming the challenges of the streak serves as an inspiring example of dedication and commitment in professional sports.

Legacy of Consistency and Durability

Cal Ripken Jr.'s consecutive games streak, which culminated at an astounding 2,632 games, has left an indelible mark on baseball history, epitomizing the virtues of consistency and durability in professional sports. This record, which Ripken set by surpassing Lou Gehrig's previously held record of 2,130 consecutive games, stands as a monumental achievement in the annals of baseball. It is not just the length of the streak that is remarkable, but also the consistent high-level performance and resilience Ripken demonstrated throughout.

The streak's significance in baseball history lies in its representation of an unwavering commitment to the game. Ripken's presence on the field, game after game, season after season, became a symbol of reliability and steadfastness. This unwavering consistency showcased not only his physical and mental resilience but also underscored his profound passion for the game of baseball. Ripken's ability to maintain a high standard of play throughout the streak, often contributing significantly to his team's performance, emphasized that his record was not merely about longevity but also about impactful participation.

Ripken's streak redefined what it means to be a durable athlete in baseball. It challenged the norms around rest and player management in the sport, highlighting the potential of what can be achieved through perseverance and careful self-management. His approach to the game, characterized by a meticulous preparation routine and a deep understanding of his own physical capabilities, set a new standard for athlete endurance in baseball.

Beyond the numbers, Ripken's streak resonates with players and fans alike as a symbol of dedication and a love for the game. His commitment to showing up for his team, no matter the circumstances, inspired countless young athletes and reinforced the value of hard work, resilience, and a team-first mentality. The legacy of Cal Ripken Jr.'s streak of consistency and durability extends beyond his personal achievements, influencing the culture of baseball and setting an inspiring example for future generations of players. It stands as a testament to the remarkable feats that can be accomplished with dedication, reliability, and a relentless pursuit of excellence.

Baseball and Civil Rights: Roberto Clemente

Early Life and Entry into Baseball

Roberto Clemente's story, intertwined with baseball and civil rights, began in his early life in Puerto Rico. Born in 1934 in Carolina, Puerto Rico, Clemente grew up in a modest setting, where his love for baseball was evident from a young age. Playing baseball using a makeshift bat and balls in the streets of his neighborhood, Clemente developed a deep passion for the game that would become his life's work. His early life in Puerto Rico laid the foundation for his strong character and determination, traits that would later define his career and humanitarian efforts.

Clemente's talent on the baseball field was apparent early on. He played amateur baseball in Puerto Rico, where his extraordinary abilities as a right fielder caught the attention of scouts from Major League Baseball. His arm strength, speed, and hitting prowess made him stand out among his peers. In 1954, at the age of 19, Clemente's journey in professional baseball began when he signed with the Brooklyn Dodgers and was assigned to their minor league team, the Montreal Royals.

Clemente's time in the minor leagues was a period of growth and development, where he honed his skills and adapted to the challenges of professional baseball. However, it was also a time when he faced significant racial and language barriers. As a Black Latino player, Clemente experienced discrimination and cultural isolation, challenges that he navigated with resilience and grace. These experiences shaped his perspective and fueled his commitment to advocating for civil rights and equality, both in baseball and beyond.

In 1955, Clemente's Major League career officially began when he joined the Pittsburgh Pirates. His entry into MLB was not just a personal achievement but a significant moment in the history of the sport, particularly as it pertained to the representation of Latino players. Clemente's early life and entry into baseball were marked by his exceptional talent and his ability to overcome adversity. His journey from the fields of Puerto Rico to the major leagues in the United States stands as a manifestation of his dedication to the game of baseball and his unwavering spirit in the face of challenges.

On-Field Excellence

Roberto Clemente's career in Major League Baseball was marked by remarkable on-field excellence, characterized by his exceptional batting prowess and outstanding defensive skills. As a right fielder for the Pittsburgh Pirates, Clemente became renowned for his powerful and accurate arm, making him one of the most feared outfielders in the game. His ability to throw out base runners from deep in the outfield with pinpoint precision was nothing short of extraordinary, earning him a reputation as one of the best defensive players of his time.

Clemente's batting was equally impressive. He was known for his aggressive and stylish batting technique, which led to consistently high batting averages throughout his career. He won the National League batting title four times and finished his career with a remarkable .317 lifetime batting average. His hitting was not just about power; it was also about finesse and timing, making him a reliable and formidable presence at the plate.

Throughout his 18-year career with the Pirates, Clemente accumulated exactly 3,000 hits, a milestone that symbolized his consistency and excellence as a hitter. This achievement made him the 11th player in MLB history to reach the 3,000-hit mark at the time. His approach to hitting was meticulous; he studied pitchers and their techniques rigorously, which helped him adjust his strategy during games and become a more effective hitter.

Beyond his individual accomplishments, Clemente was a key player in leading the Pittsburgh Pirates to success, including two World Series championships in 1960 and 1971. In the 1971 World Series, Clemente's performance was particularly outstanding, earning him the World Series Most Valuable Player (MVP) award. His performance in the postseason was evidence of his ability to excel under pressure and contribute significantly to his team's success.

Clemente's on-field achievements were a reflection of his extraordinary talent and dedication to the game of baseball. His batting prowess and defensive skills not only earned him numerous accolades, including 12 Gold Glove Awards and 15 All-Star game appearances but also endeared him to fans and garnered respect among his peers. Roberto Clemente's excellence on the baseball field is remembered as one of the hallmarks of his legacy, showcasing the skill, passion, and work ethic that made him one of the greatest players in the history of the sport.

Advocacy and Impact

Roberto Clemente's impact extended far beyond the baseball field, as he was also a passionate advocate for civil rights and equality. His experiences as a Black Latino player in Major League Baseball during a time of significant racial and ethnic tensions deeply influenced his perspective and actions regarding social justice issues. Clemente was not one to shy away from speaking out against discrimination and injustice, both in the context of baseball and in the broader societal framework.

Within the realm of baseball, Clemente was a vocal advocate for Latino players. He often spoke about the challenges they faced, including language barriers, cultural isolation, and racial discrimination. His status as a star player gave him a platform, which he used effectively to raise awareness about these issues. Clemente pushed for better treatment and more inclusive policies for Latino players in MLB, paving the way for future generations.

Clemente's advocacy work extended into his personal life and community involvement. He was deeply committed to humanitarian efforts, particularly in his native Puerto Rico and other Latin American countries. Clemente frequently organized and participated in charity events, using his fame to draw attention to the needs of the less fortunate. His humanitarian efforts were not just limited to financial aid; he was actively involved on the ground, often delivering baseball equipment and other supplies to those in need.

One of the most significant aspects of Clemente's impact was his role as a bridge between different communities. He was revered in both the United States and Latin America, bringing attention to the shared experiences of these communities and fostering a sense of unity. Clemente's dedication to civil rights and equality was a central part of his legacy, demonstrating that athletes can play a crucial role in advocating for social change.

Through his actions and words, Roberto Clemente established himself as more than just an outstanding baseball player; he was a humanitarian and a champion for social justice. His commitment to advocating for civil rights and equality left a lasting impact on baseball and society, solidifying his place as an influential and respected figure in the fight against discrimination and for the betterment of underprivileged communities. Clemente's legacy as an advocate for social change continues to inspire and resonate with people around the world, highlighting the power of using one's platform for the greater good.

Legacy of Humanitarianism

Roberto Clemente's legacy as a humanitarian and role model is as profound as his legacy as a baseball player. His commitment to helping others, particularly those in need in his native Puerto Rico and other Latin American countries, defined much of his life off the field. His dedication to humanitarian causes was rooted in his deep sense of empathy and his desire to use his status as a public figure to make a positive impact on the world.

Clemente's humanitarian work was varied and extensive. He was involved in numerous charity events and initiatives, often focusing on helping children and the underprivileged. He organized baseball clinics, donated sports equipment, and was always ready to lend a helping hand to those in need. His efforts were not just about providing financial support but also about being physically present and involved in these communities. Clemente believed in the power of personal engagement and the importance of giving back, principles that guided much of his humanitarian work.

Tragically, Clemente's life and career were cut short in a plane crash on December 31, 1972, while he was on a mission to deliver aid to earthquake victims in Nicaragua. This selfless act was a reflection of his character and his commitment to humanitarian causes. His untimely death was a profound loss, not only to the world of baseball but also to the countless people he had helped and inspired through his off-field endeavors.

Clemente's legacy of humanitarianism has continued to inspire generations after his passing. He is remembered not only as one of the greatest baseball players but also as a compassionate and dedicated humanitarian. His legacy is celebrated each year in MLB with the Roberto Clemente Award, given to a player who exemplifies sportsmanship and community involvement, echoing Clemente's own values and contributions.

Roberto Clemente's impact as a role model extends beyond his humanitarian efforts. He demonstrated how athletes can use their platform for the greater good, inspiring others to engage in social causes and make a difference in their communities. His legacy as a humanitarian and role model is a vital part of his enduring influence, serving as a reminder of the powerful role athletes can play in society, beyond their achievements in sports. Clemente's commitment to helping others and his tragic death while doing so have cemented his status as an icon of altruism and a true hero both on and off the baseball field.

Babe Ruth's Inspiring Journey

Challenging Childhood

Babe Ruth's journey to becoming one of baseball's greatest legends began with a challenging childhood in Baltimore, Maryland. Born George Herman Ruth Jr. in 1895, Ruth faced a tumultuous early life that significantly influenced his path to baseball stardom. His childhood was marked by poverty and hardship, growing up in a rough neighborhood where survival often took precedence over schooling and childhood play.

Ruth's parents, struggling to make ends meet and manage their large family, found it increasingly difficult to control their son's rebellious behavior. This led to his placement at St. Mary's Industrial School for Boys, a reformatory and orphanage, at the age of seven. The strict discipline and regimented structure of St. Mary's were a stark contrast to the freedom and chaos of his life in Baltimore's streets. However, it was at St. Mary's that Ruth found his refuge and calling in baseball.

At St. Mary's, Ruth was under the guidance of Brother Matthias Boutlier, a disciplinarian yet caring figure who introduced him to baseball. Brother Matthias recognized Ruth's natural talent for the game and became his mentor, nurturing his abilities as a player. Ruth quickly excelled in baseball, showing an early aptitude for both pitching and batting. The sport provided a positive outlet for his energy and a focus for his ambitions, setting him on a path that would lead him away from the hardships of his early life.

Ruth's time at St. Mary's was more than just an escape from his troubled upbringing; it was a foundational period that shaped his future. The discipline he learned at the school, combined with the baseball skills he developed, prepared him for the challenges and opportunities that lay ahead. This period of his life instilled in him the perseverance, determination, and passion for baseball that would become the hallmarks of his legendary career. Ruth's challenging childhood and the transformative years at St. Mary's Industrial School for Boys were crucial in molding the young boy into the sports icon he would eventually become.

Rise to Stardom

Babe Ruth's rise to stardom in professional baseball is a story of extraordinary talent and transformation. His journey to becoming one of the most iconic figures in the sport began with his entry into professional baseball, which was marked by an early demonstration of his remarkable skills. Ruth started his professional career as a pitcher for the Baltimore Orioles of the International League, where his abilities on the mound quickly garnered attention. However, it was his move to the Boston Red Sox in 1914 that marked the beginning of his rise in Major League Baseball.

With the Red Sox, Ruth's talents as a pitcher flourished. He was known for his powerful left arm, delivering pitches with speed and accuracy that made him one of the top pitchers in the league. His pitching prowess helped lead the Red Sox to three World Series titles in 1915, 1916, and 1918. Despite his success as a pitcher, it was Ruth's potential at the plate that set him apart. He began to show an exceptional ability for hitting, which would eventually lead to a dramatic shift in his baseball career.

Ruth's transformation into a legendary hitter began in earnest with his move to the New York Yankees in 1920. This change marked a significant turning point in his career and the sport of baseball. With the Yankees, Ruth transitioned from being a pitcher to an outfielder, allowing him to focus more on batting. His impact as a hitter was immediate and profound. Ruth's home runs were not just frequent; they were majestic, often traveling extraordinary distances. His ability to hit home runs changed the way the game was played, making it more exciting and drawing more fans to the sport.

Ruth's time with the Yankees saw him shatter multiple batting records, including the most home runs in a single season and the most career home runs. His charisma and larger-than-life personality, combined with his unprecedented skills at the plate, made him a national celebrity. Ruth's rise to stardom was not just about his transformation from a pitcher to a hitter; it was about revolutionizing baseball, making it a sport of power and spectacle. His entry into professional baseball and subsequent success with the Boston Red Sox and transformation with the New York Yankees is a testament to his unparalleled talent and enduring impact on the sport.

Record-Breaking Achievements

Babe Ruth's career in baseball is synonymous with record-breaking achievements, particularly in the realm of home run hitting. His impact on the game and the New York Yankees was monumental, changing the nature of baseball and capturing the imagination of fans across the nation. Ruth's ability to hit home runs with stunning frequency and distance transformed him into a baseball legend and altered the way the game was played and perceived.

Ruth's home run records are a cornerstone of his legacy. In 1920, his first year with the Yankees, he hit a staggering 54 home runs, more than any other team in the American League that year. This feat was not a one-off occurrence; Ruth consistently led the league in home runs, including hitting a then-unprecedented 60 home runs in the 1927 season. This record stood for 34 years, evidence of Ruth's extraordinary power at the plate. His career total of 714 home runs was a record that remained unbroken for decades, underscoring his dominance in this aspect of the game.

Beyond his individual records, Ruth's impact on the New York Yankees' successes was profound. He helped the team win seven American League pennants and four World Series titles. His presence in the lineup made the Yankees a formidable team, feared by pitchers and admired by fans. Ruth's ability to draw crowds and generate excitement about the game contributed significantly to the team's financial success and popularity.

Ruth's influence extended beyond his statistical achievements; he changed the game of baseball itself. Before Ruth, baseball was largely a game of strategy, focused on bunting, stealing bases, and singles. Ruth introduced the concept of power-hitting, making home runs a central and thrilling part of the game. His style of play captivated fans and inspired future generations of players, shifting the focus of baseball from a low-scoring, strategic game to one characterized by power and excitement.

Babe Ruth's record-breaking achievements in home run hitting and his impact on the Yankees and baseball as a whole are integral to his enduring legacy. He transformed the sport with his exceptional talent, reshaping baseball into America's beloved pastime. Ruth's influence on the game is still felt today, and his records and approach to baseball continue to be a benchmark and inspiration in the sport.

Off-Field Impact and Legacy

Babe Ruth's influence extended well beyond the baseball diamond, characterized by his larger-than-life personality and his significant charitable endeavors. Off the field, Ruth was known for his charismatic and gregarious nature, which endeared him to fans and made him a cultural icon of his time. His love for the game and joyous approach to life resonated with the public, making him one of the most beloved figures in the history of American sports.

Ruth's charitable work was a significant aspect of his off-field activities. He had a soft spot for children, often visiting hospitals and orphanages, where he would spend time with young fans. Ruth's generosity was not just limited to his time; he was also known for his financial contributions to various charities and causes. His involvement in charity work was driven by a deep sense of empathy and a desire to give back to the community, particularly to those less fortunate.

Beyond his charitable actions, Ruth's legacy as a public figure was marked by the way he handled fame. Despite his superstar status, he remained approachable and relatable, often interacting with fans and the media in a candid and jovial manner. This accessibility and genuine nature contributed significantly to his popularity and enduring legacy.

Ruth's legacy as one of baseball's greatest icons is undisputed. He revolutionized the sport with his extraordinary skills and changed how it was played and perceived. His name became synonymous with baseball greatness, inspiring future generations of players and fans alike. Ruth's impact on the game of baseball and American culture was profound, making him not just a sports hero but also a cultural icon.

Babe Ruth's off-field impact, combined with his unparalleled achievements in baseball, cemented his status as a legend in the truest sense. His enduring legacy is evident in the continued admiration and reverence he receives, decades after his passing. Ruth's larger-than-life personality, his charitable endeavors, and his contributions to baseball have ensured that his memory lives on, not just as a phenomenal athlete but as a symbol of joy, generosity, and the enduring spirit of America's pastime.

References

Biography.com editors. *Babe Ruth*. Biography.com (2014). https://www.biography.com/athletes/babe-ruth. Accessed December 05, 2023.

Borgemenke, Ryan. *Joe Nuxhall*. Society for American Baseball Research (20). https://sabr.org/bioproj/person/joe-nuxhall/. Accessed December 01, 2023.

Campbell, Jim. *Cal Ripken, Jr.* Chelsea House (2015).

Fanucchi, David. *Miracle on Grass: How Hall of Famer Tommy Lasorda Led Team USA to a Shocking Upset Over Cuba, Capturing the Only Olympic Gold Medal in USA Baseball History.* CreateSpace Independent Publishing Platform (2012).

Larsen, Don and Shaw, Mark. *The Perfect Yankee: The Incredible Story of the Greatest Miracle in Baseball History.* Sports Publishing (2012).

Markusen, Bruce. *Roberto Clemente: The Great One.* Sports Publishing (2014).

Newberry, Paul. *A timeline of Hank Aaron's life and career.* Boston.com (2021). https://www.boston.com/sports/mlb/2021/01/23/timeline-hank-aaron-life-career/. Accessed November 29, 2023

Swaine, Rick. *Jackie Robinson.* Society for American Baseball Research (2012). https://sabr.org/bioproj/person/jackie-robinson/. Accessed December 03, 2023

Bonus: Free Book!

Are you ready to delve into the thrilling book in the series, absolutely free? Get ready to go deep into the world of yet another football legend! Just use your smartphone or tablet to scan the QR code below, then follow the simple prompts to receive the PDF.

www.ingramcontent.com/pod-product-compliance
Lightning Source LLC
Chambersburg PA
CBHW052104110526
44591CB00013B/2346